The Christmas S
from the *Read With Me*

CANDLE BOOKS

Mary and the Angel
Luke 1

God sent an angel to Mary, who was a virgin.
She was preparing to marry a man named Joseph.
The angel went to Mary and said,
"Greetings. God is with you."
Mary was very troubled.
But the angel said, "Don't be afraid, Mary,
you have found favour with God.
You will give birth to a son.
You are to give him the name Jesus."

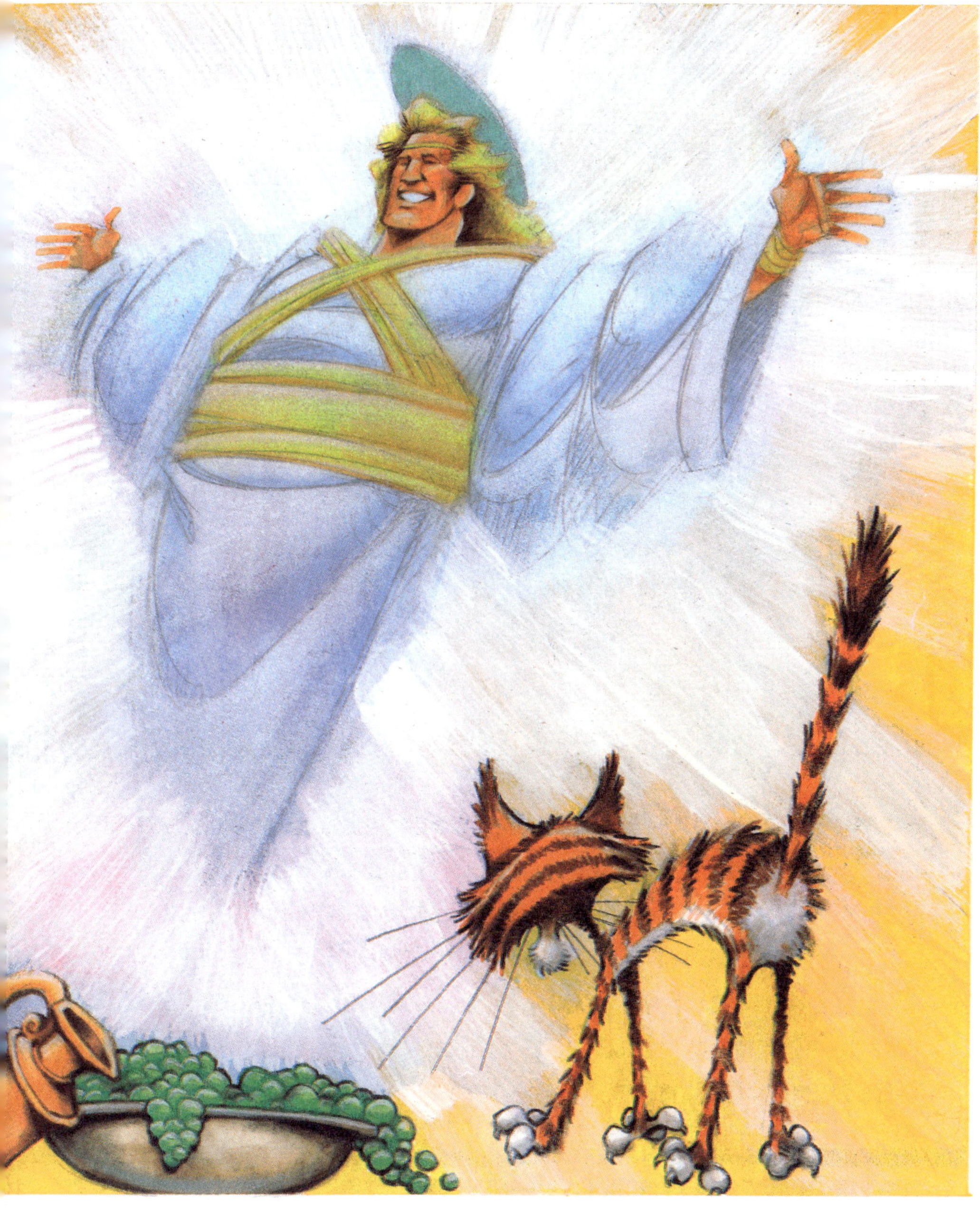

"How will this be?" Mary asked.
The angel answered, "The Holy Spirit will come upon you. The holy one to be born will be called the Son of God.
Nothing is impossible with God."

"I am God's servant," Mary answered.
"May all this happen to me just as you have said."
Then the angel left.

Jesus Is Born
Luke 2

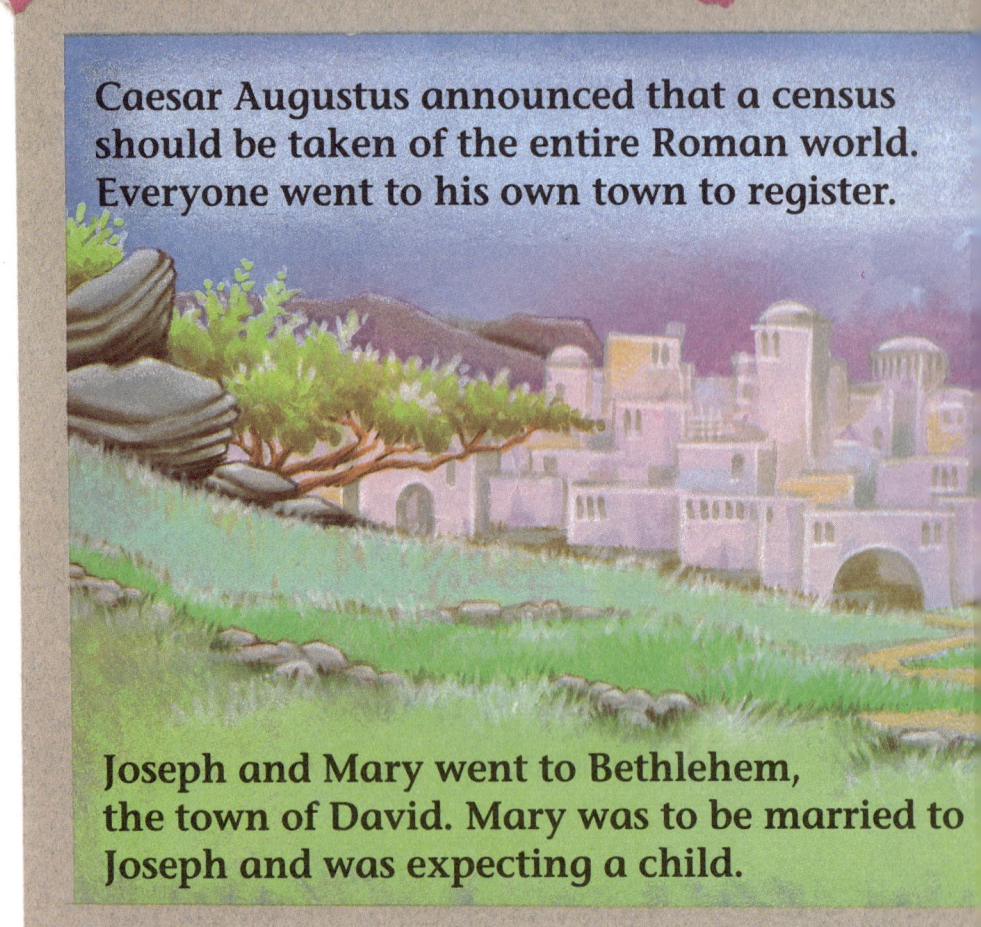

Caesar Augustus announced that a census should be taken of the entire Roman world. Everyone went to his own town to register.

Joseph and Mary went to Bethlehem, the town of David. Mary was to be married to Joseph and was expecting a child.

7

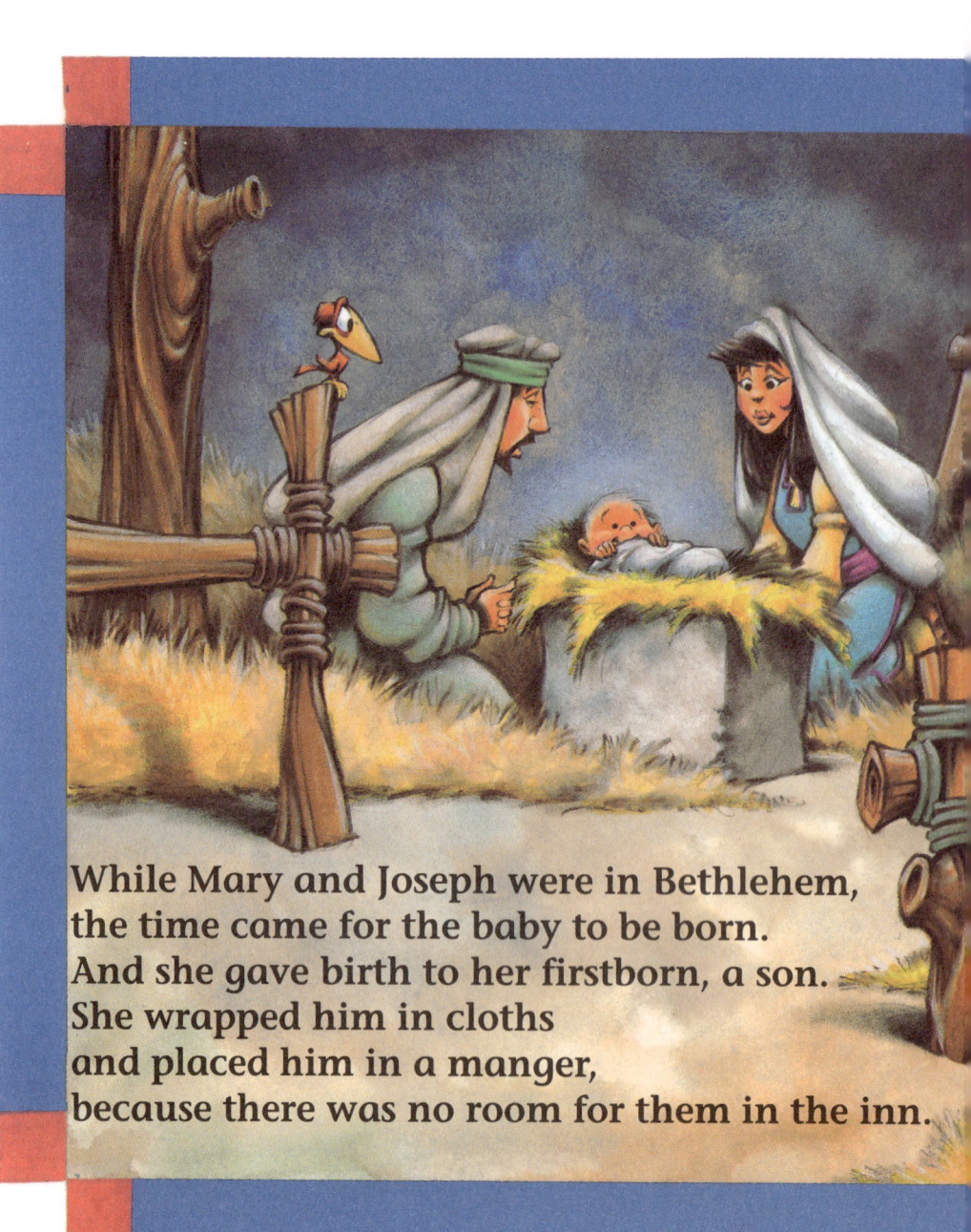

While Mary and Joseph were in Bethlehem,
the time came for the baby to be born.
And she gave birth to her firstborn, a son.
She wrapped him in cloths
and placed him in a manger,
because there was no room for them in the inn.

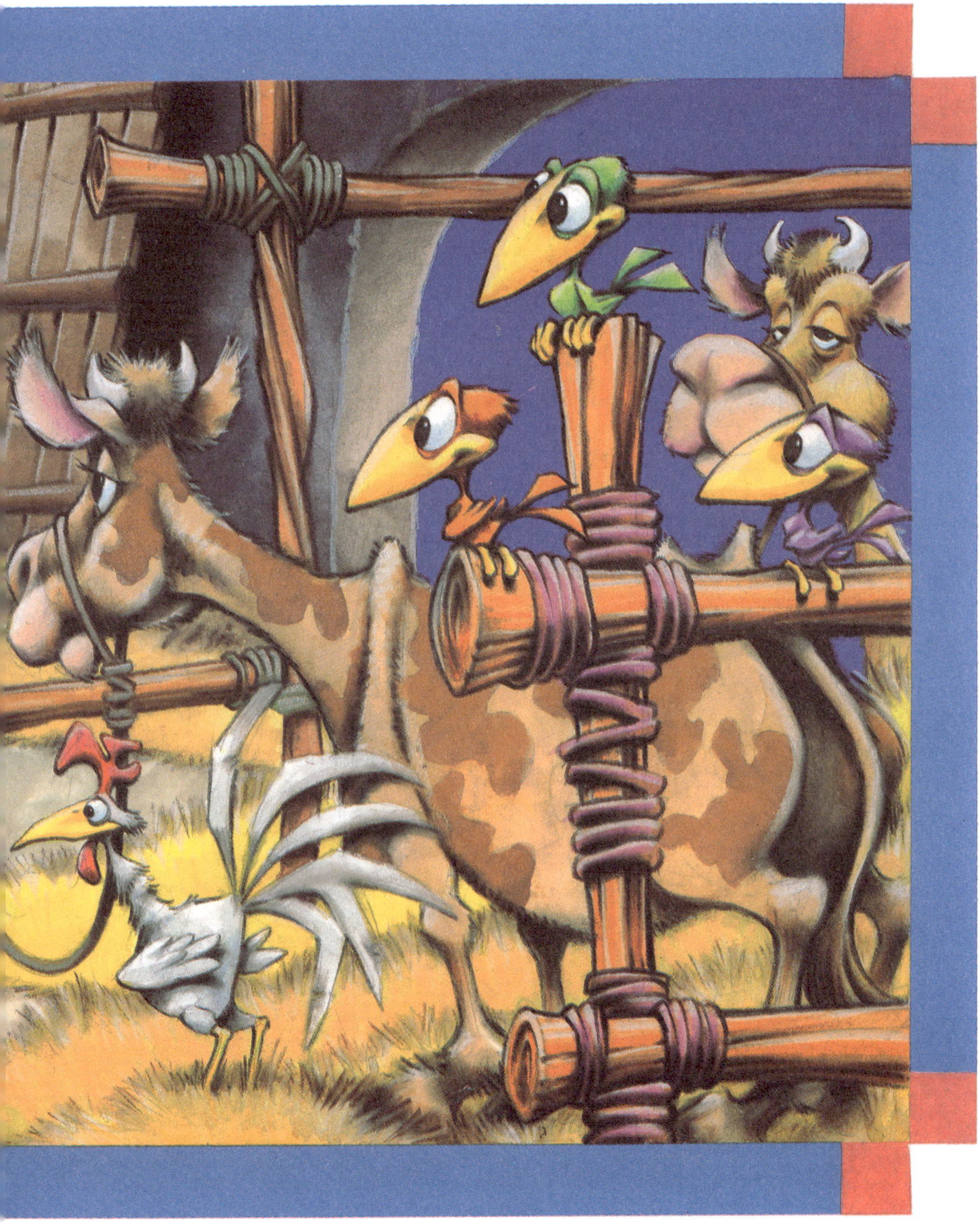

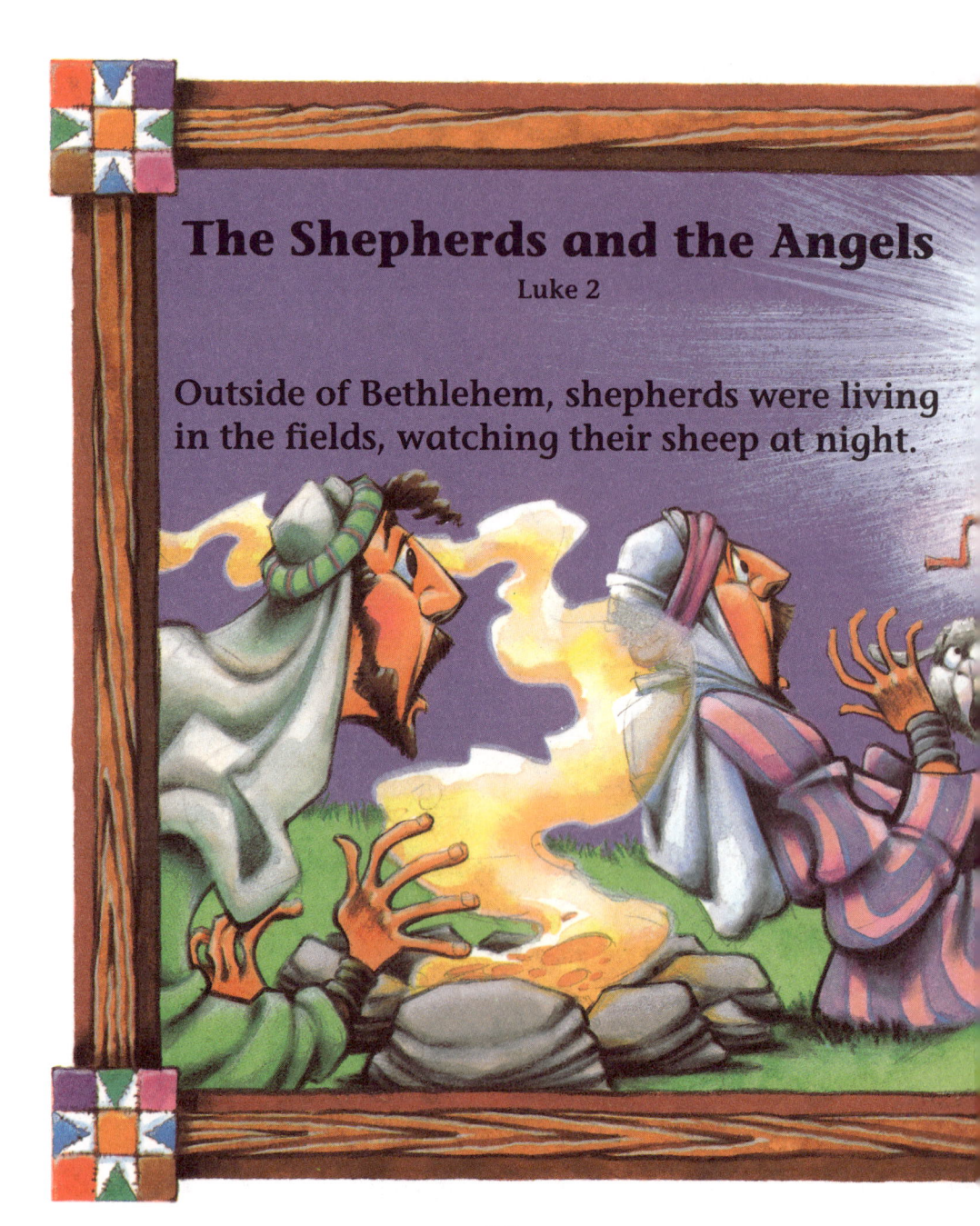

The Shepherds and the Angels
Luke 2

Outside of Bethlehem, shepherds were living in the fields, watching their sheep at night.

An angel of God appeared to the shepherds.
The glory of God shone around them.
And they were afraid.

But the angel said to them, "Don't be afraid.
I bring you good news of great joy
that will be for all the people.
Today in Bethlehem a Saviour has been born.
He is Christ the Lord. You will find a baby
wrapped in cloths and lying in a manger."

Suddenly many, many angels appeared,
praising God and saying,
"Glory to God in the highest, and on earth peace."

When the angels had left them, the shepherds hurried to Bethlehem.

They found Mary and Joseph and the baby, who was lying in the manger.

When they had seen the baby Jesus,
they told everyone about him.
And everyone who heard the story
was amazed at what the shepherds said.

The Magi Visit Jesus
Matthew 2

After Jesus was born in Bethlehem,
Magi from the east came to Jerusalem.
"Where is the one who has been born
king of the Jews?" they asked.
"We saw his star in the east.
We have come to worship him."

17

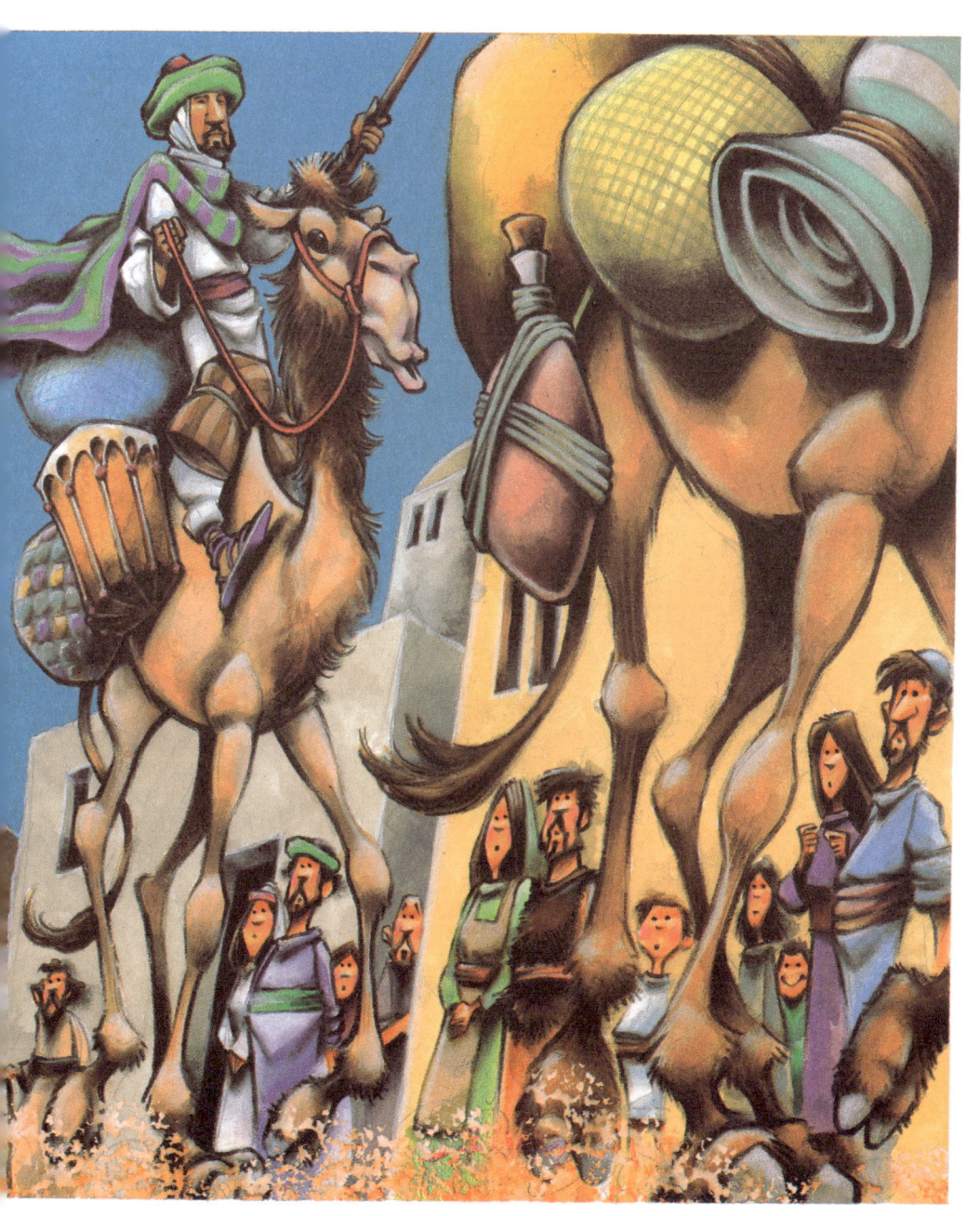

When King Herod heard this he was upset.

He called the Magi secretly and found out the exact time the star had appeared.

He sent them to Bethlehem and said, "Make a careful search for the child. As soon as you find him, report to me, so that I too may go and worship him."

The Magi went on their way.
The star went ahead of the Magi until it stopped over the place where the child lived.
When they saw the star they were overjoyed.

Coming to the house, they saw
Jesus with his mother Mary.
They bowed down and worshipped him.
Then they presented him with gifts of gold
and of incense and of myrrh.

God told them in a dream not to go back to Herod.
And they returned to their country by another way.

The Escape to Egypt
Matthew 2

When the Magi had gone,
an angel appeared to Joseph in a dream.
"Get up," he said, "take the child and
his mother and escape to Egypt.
Stay there until I tell you, for Herod is
going to search for the child to kill him."

So Joseph got up, took Jesus and his mother during the night and left for Egypt.
They stayed there until the death of Herod.

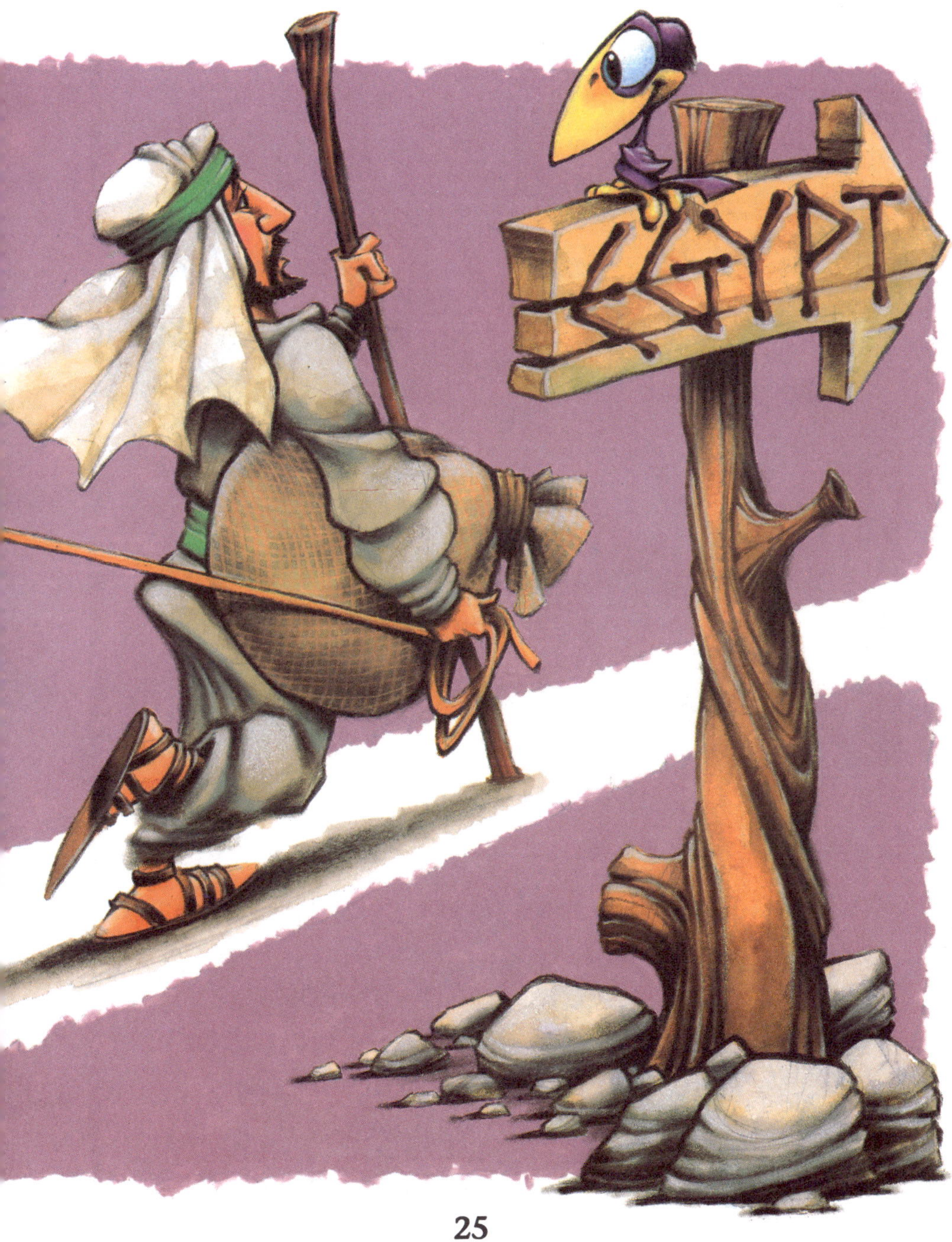
EGYPT

The Boy Jesus at the Temple
Luke 2

When Jesus was twelve years old,
he went with Mary and Joseph
to Jerusalem for the Passover Feast.
When the Feast was over, they went home.
But Jesus stayed behind in Jerusalem.
His parents didn't know about it.

They thought he was in their company,
so Mary and Joseph travelled for a day.
Then they began to look for him.
When they couldn't find him, they went back
to Jerusalem to look for him.

After three days Mary and Joseph
found Jesus in the temple.
He was sitting with the teachers,
listening to them and asking them questions.
Everyone who heard Jesus was amazed
at his understanding and his answers.

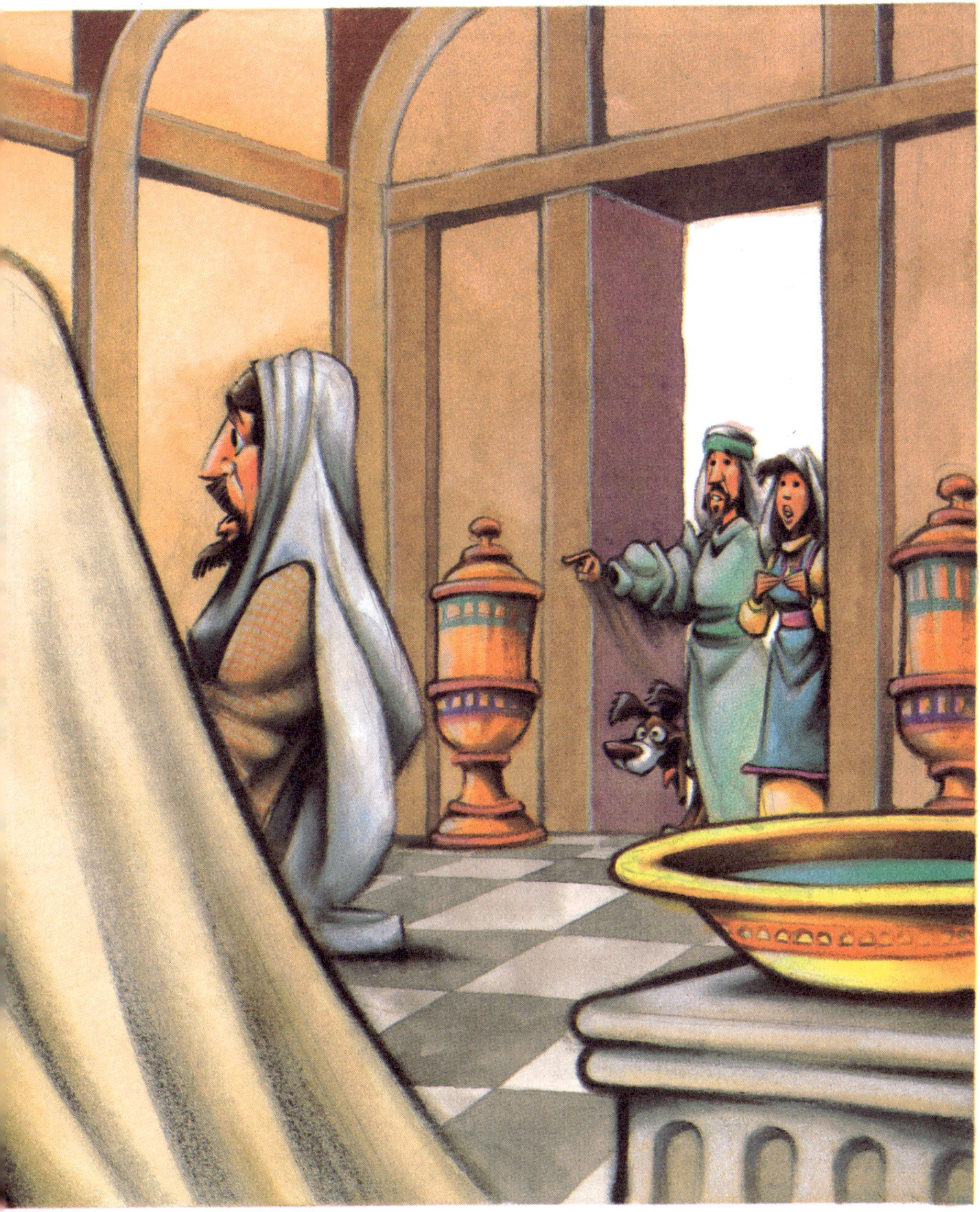

When Jesus' parents saw him, they were surprised.
His mother said, "Son, why have you
treated us like this? Your father and I
have been anxiously searching for you."
"Why were you searching for me?" he asked.
"Didn't you know I had to be
in my Father's house?"
But Mary and Joseph did not
understand what he was saying.

Then Jesus went home with Mary and Joseph and obeyed them. He grew in wisdom and stature, and in favour with God and men.

The Christmas Story

Illustrated by Dennis Jones
Edited by Doris Rikkers and Jean E. Syswerda

READ WITH ME BIBLE
Copyright © 1993 by the Zondervan Corporation

Scripture portions adapted from The Holy Bible,
New International Version
Copyright © 1973, 1978, 1984 by International Bible Society

The 'NIV' and 'New International Version' trademarks are registered in the United States Patent and Trademark Office by International Bible Society.

All rights reserved. No part of this publication may be reproduced, stored in a retrieval system, or transmitted in any form or by any means – electronic, mechanical, photocopy, recording or any other – except for brief quotations in printed reviews, without the prior permission of the publisher.

ISBN 1 85985 192 4
Published in the UK by Candle Books 1998
Distributed by STL
PO Box 300, Carlisle,
CA3 0QS

Worldwide coedition organised and produced by Angus Hudson Ltd, Concorde House, Grenville Place, Mill Hill, London NW7 3SA, England
Tel: +44 181 959 3668
Fax: +44 181 959 3678

Printed in England